For Dad
and Mum

G.S.

First published 1993
by Walker Books Ltd
87 Vauxhall Walk, London SE11 5HJ

Text © 1993 Jan Mark
Illustrations © 1993 Gay Shephard

This book has been typeset in Calligraphic

Printed and bound in Italy by
L.E.G.O., Vicenza

British Library Cataloguing in Publication Data
A catalogue record for this book is
available from the British Library.

ISBN 0-7445-2190-4

This Bowl of Earth

Written by

Jan Mark

Illustrated by

Gay Shephard

WALKER BOOKS
LONDON

*S*ome people grow flowers in the garden. Some people grow vegetables. Some people grow shrubs. I grow roses and shrubs and trees. Four years ago there was nothing but grass in my garden. One day it will be full of trees.

Some plants grow up in a few weeks. Some take months. Trees take years to grow. That is why they are special.

A shrub is a bush.

Sometimes I go to the garden centre and buy a little tree. Sometimes I stick a twig in the earth. And sometimes the twig will grow.

This little birch tree came from the garden centre. It grew from a seed.

Some seeds are so small they look like dust. Some are very large.

This willow tree is a quickset: it grew from a live twig.

"Quick" means "alive". The "quick" of your fingernail is the part that is joined to your finger, still growing.

By the back step are some
big flowerpots. I grow bushes in them.
The bushes are happy here. Near the house it is always
warmer than down in the garden. The central heating
vent is close by. Beside the drain is a bowl of earth.
Last year I grew bulbs in it.

Today I went for a walk and
saw a garrya bush by the roadside.
In spring the garrya has very long catkins,
as long as the tail on Charlie, our cat. I
have always wanted a garrya bush, so I
picked a twig, no more, just a twig,
as long as my finger.

pussy willow
catkin

silver birch
catkin

alder catkin

Catkins are
clusters of flowers
full of pollen.
They do not look
like violets or roses
but they are
flowers all the same.

When I came home I pushed the twig into the bowl of earth by the back step. The earth is warm and damp. It is May, and all the plants in the garden are growing. Perhaps the twig will grow.

Now it is June and
I have been to stay with
a friend. She has a big
garden, bigger than mine.
It has a pond with frogs,
and trees and bushes.
One of the bushes is a
pink jasmine, and one is
a yellow buddleia. I like
buddleia bushes and so
do butterflies.

buddleia

This kind
of jasmine is a climbing
plant. It likes to grow
over a trellis.

I asked my friend
for some twigs
and when I came
home I stuck them
in the bowl of earth,
beside the garrya.

*S*ometimes July is wet
and chilly, but this year
it is hot and dry. It has not
rained for weeks. Every day I
water the plants in the garden
and the bushes in the
flowerpots. And I water
the bowl of earth.

August is almost over and
still it has not rained. I keep
on watering the garden,
and the flowerpots, and the
bowl of earth. The jasmine
is growing. The garrya is
losing its leaves. I think it
is dead but I may be wrong.
The buddleia twigs are too
big now for the bowl of earth.
I take them out and put one in a pot for a
friend. I put one in a pot for my mother.
One is for me. I plant it in the garden.
It has a flower·bud on it.

Plants ought to be watered
in the morning, before the sun is
high, or after it has set.

At last it has rained.
In September the nights
are cold but the bowl of earth
is warm, down by the back step,
near the central heating vent.
The air is damp too, because of
the drain. In the garden the
yellow buddleia has flowered.
Butterflies visit it. So do bees.
Three months ago it was a twig.
Now it is a little tree.

Buddleia grows so fast that
it needs to be cut back every year.

In the front garden is a pussy willow tree.
I grew it from a twig. Today I pruned it.
I cut off the ends of the branches so that
they will grow strong and healthy next year.
I put some of the cuttings in a vase.
I put some in the bowl of earth.

*O*ctober nights can be frosty,
but it is warm and damp in the
bowl of earth. Roots are growing.
The jasmine is alive. The garrya
has lost all its leaves but I shall
keep it a bit longer … just in case.

November is cold. Nothing grows in the garden. Plants rest in winter time. But it is still warm in the bowl of earth. Today I went to the bookshop in town. Near the bookshop is a spindle tree with beautiful berries, orange and pink.

I want a tree like that, so I asked for a twig, no more, just a twig, as long as my thumb, and brought it home. I put it in the bowl of earth.

There is a surprise plant in the bowl of earth. The people next door have an elder tree in the garden. Birds like elderberries and take them to eat. Sometimes they drop them. A bird must have dropped an elderberry into my bowl of earth because now there is a little elder tree growing there. Good. I've always wanted an elder tree.

Some plants keep their leaves in winter. They are called evergreens. Holly and ivy are evergreens. So are Christmas trees.

*T*oday it snowed a little, but plants don't mind snow. In the bowl of earth the jasmine and the elder are alive. The spindle twig has leaves and berries. The pussy willow is alive. I'm sure the garrya is dead. We have bought holly for Christmas. A little piece fell off, so I stuck it in the bowl of earth, but I don't think it will grow.

A new year has begun. There is another surprise in the bowl of earth. Green shoots are growing among the twigs. I forgot to take the bulbs out of the earth last year, when the flowers died, and now they are growing again. I wonder what they will be.

February is very cold this year. The earth in the garden is frozen day and night, but not the earth in the bowl. All my twigs have buds on, except the garrya. Now it has snowed. It snowed so hard last night that all the garden is white. I cannot see the bowl of earth at all. It is just a white hump by the white step.

One twig sticks out.
It is the jasmine.
The frost has cracked
some of the flowerpots.
It has not cracked
the bowl of earth,
but what will happen
to my twigs?

Plants that can live through
frost are called "hardy".
Snowdrops are hardy.
Dahlias are not.

The snow melted.
All the twigs are alive
and growing –
except the garrya, and
that was dead already. Next month
I shall take them out of the bowl of earth
and plant them in the garden. Next time
I go for a walk I shall pick another
garrya twig and try again.

At Easter I planted all
my other twigs in the garden.
They are beginning to grow
taller. There is nothing
left in the bowl of earth
except the bulbs.

A bulb is a whole plant packed small.

The green spikes are quite big now. The frost and snow did not hurt them. I think they are going to be tulips. Next month I shall know.

The word "tulip" means "turban".
Think about this ...
          next time you see a tulip.

Index

*Look up the pages to find out about
all these garden things. Don't forget
to look at both kinds of words:
this kind and **this kind**.*